UNDERGRAD

undergrad

A COMMONPLACE BOOK

Laila El Mugammar

Laila El Mugammar

Copyright © 2021 by Laila El Mugammar

All rights reserved. No part of this book may be reproduced in any manner whatsoever without written permission except in the case of brief quotations embodied in critical articles and reviews.

to Cheryl

Contents

Dedication		v
foreword		ix
essays		**1**
1	"Oh, How She Did Suffer"	2
2	On Tampons, the Archive, and the Menses Bildungsroman	15
3	"Where Youse Belong"	20
4	On Contact Zones, Safe Houses, and the Ahmed Mohamed Clock Incident	25
5	On "Brokeback Mountain"	32
6	On Queer Shame And Serophobia in Fight Club	40
creative nonfiction		**47**
7	On Intersectionality	48

8	On University Librarians	52
9	On Canada	56
10	Critical Mass	59
11	"Keep The Volume Low"	63
12	On Fried Chicken, Disordered Eating, and Storytelling	69
13	On Cultural Renaissance	74
14	On New Orleans	78

fiction — 83

15	The Body	84

Works Cited — 91
Acknowledgments — 95
About The Author — 96

foreword

this is just to say
i have almost no respect for the English language
and what I do have left in this icebox
i am saving for people's pronouns.
forgive me
they are wonderful
so sweet
and so warm
- Laila *(she/her/hers)*

essays

1

"Oh, How She Did Suffer"

ON DISPLACEMENT AND CONTESTATION IN THE BLACK AND INDIGENOUS WESTERN

In her introduction to *Westerns: A Women's History*, Victoria Lamont suggests that most popular western women's writers were complicit in "frontier club colonialism," noting that "Curtis, McElrath, and Bower accepted the displacement of Indigenous peoples as an inevitability and were less concerned with racial conflicts between Indigenous people and white settlers than they were with class tensions within settler communities" (Lamont p. 6). When Black and Indigenous writing is introduced, the idea of displacement as an inevitability is complicated. Sarah Winnemucca's memoir *Life Among The Piutes: Their Wrongs and Claims* reveals the brutality of enacting displacement in practice, in her history of the Piutes of the Great Basin region (1). Winnemucca's exposition of displacement as laborious and detrimental contests its inevitability. Black voices are largely absent from the Western, and Pauline Hopkins' *Winona: A Tale Of Negro Life in the South and Southwest* allows for an emergent history of Black displacement, and subsequent placemaking in the American West. Although both texts map displacement as a result of the colonial process, displacement is coterminous with suffering for the Piutes while it is a product of agency and a welcome respite from slavery for Winona, Judah, and White Eagle.

As an Indigenous author writing in a European parochial context, Sarah Winnemucca's writing was subject to colonialist criticism. As an ethnohistorical autobiography, *Life Among The Piutes* is subject to expectations of objective truth. Winnemucca maps displacement as the source of pain and suffering resulting from conquest, and from the Westward expansion of the United States. *Life Among the Piutes* was written "for political purposes: to inform her White audience about the injustices of the reservation system and to raise money for the impoverished Paiutes" (Lape 259-20). Though the text is nonfiction, it employs certain rhetoric to support these goals. The Aristotelian modes of persuasion—*ethos*, *pathos*, and *logos*—work in tandem in the text to contest the "benevolent project" of displacement.

The *logos* mode of persuasion appeals to logic, rather than emotion, in order to support the argument of the speaker. Winnemucca employs this to deconstruct the idea of Western expansion as a civilizing mission:

> Right here, my dear reader, you will see how much

> Father Wilbur's Indians are civilized and Christianized. He had to have interpreters. If they were so much civilized, why did he have interpreters to talk to them? In eighteen years could he not have taught them some English? I was there twelve months, and I never heard an Indian man or woman speak the English language except the three interpreters and some half-breeds. Could he not have had the young people taught in all that time?" (Winnemucca 214)

Winnemucca addresses the imagined reader explicitly, and by doing so, enters into a simulated dialectic. Her repetitive questions directed at the reader invite them to engage, and this invitation gives them the opportunity to contest her claims. If after "eighteen years" of living in displacement, the majority of the Piutes do not speak English for a period spanning at least twelve months, the colonial project has failed in its supposed mission of "[civilizing] and [Christianizing]" them. Her questions are anticipatory of the reader's assumed criticisms, which reflects a rhetorical strategy known as the "prebuttal." In this passage, Winnemucca successfully challenges the didactic benevolence of displacement.

Winnemucca's liminality as an interpreter must be addressed as a form of displacement: her literacy leaves her figuratively displaced from her predominantly oral culture and literally displaced as she leaves the Yakima Reservation to lecture on the East Coast about government policies and reservation corruption. As a result, "her people are suspicious of her supposed loyalty to them because she is linguistically of both nations" (Lape 266). Lape cites Victor Turner's theory of liminality, positing Winnemucca exists "betwixt and between the positions assigned and arrayed by law, custom, convention, and ceremonial" (Lape 260). This makes her voice inherently compromised: to the settler critics who accuse her of deception, and to her fellow Piutes. She addresses this compromise directly to her people, saying "I know I have told you more lies than I have hair on my head [...] I have never told you my own words; they were the words of the white people, not mine" (Winnemucca 236). Winnemucca's claim that she has never told the Piutes her own words reveals how little agency she has as a mouthpiece for white settlers, and how her role jeopardizes her status in the community. The fragility of her status is furthered when she "[reports] to the army officers" on behalf of Chief Egan that the Piutes "are all starving under this Christian man", Agent Reinhard (Winnemucca 142). Agent Reinhard immediately fires Winnemucca from her post as interpreter in retaliation, effectively silencing not only her but all of the Piutes. This event demonstrates that her voice can only be used to further the colonial project, not contest it. By including this narrative, Winnemucca contests the benevolence of the colonial project by proving that there is no recourse or accountability for Indian agents, who rule tyrannically with unchecked power.

In a work of nonfiction with clear political goals such as *Life Among the Piutes,* it appears counterintuitive for a narrator to admit she "[tells] more lies than [she has] hair on her head" (236). This would go against the *ethos* mode of persuasion, which involves appearing credible. However, Winemmucca makes clear that the lies were "the words of the white people, not mine," effectively undermining the *ethos* of the colonial enterprise that uses her to transmit the lies (236). She has established two conditions: the colonial project forces her to lie unwittingly, and the colonial project will not allow her to criticize or undermine it by speaking in her own voice. *Life Among The Piutes* is highly critical of colonialism, which introduces the probability that Winnemucca is speaking in her own voice in the memoir, and the first-person perspective supports this. The reader is provided countless examples of colonizers lying, but how can they be assured that Winnemucca herself is credible? The clearest example of *ethos* in this work lays outside the diegesis of the text. Winnemucca, likely anticipating that the veracity of her memoir would be challenged, provides an appendix with numerous letters from the Office of Indian Affairs, the Office of War, and various military personnel. The letters attest to her "exemplary" character, support the veracity of her claims, and accuse her detractors of ad feminam attacks. These letters provide the necessary *ethos* and reaffirm her voice.

Jacquelynn Kleist posits that *Life Among The Piutes* should be read as a captivity narrative. Because the text is nonfiction and does not conform neatly to settler or Indigenous literary traditions, it is itself displaced in Western literature. The captivity narrative is a recognizable genre of displacement: it involves removal from "cultural social norms and way of life" (Kleist 79). Suffering at the hands of ethnically distinct captors is a key part of Winnemucca's text, as is a physical exile from the homeland. Winnemucca subverts the traditional genre of "Indian captivity narrative" which involves white settler women captured and brutalized by Indigenous men. This relies on the exclusion of Indigenous voices, and Winnemucca's story resists this by centering Indigenous perspectives. "Indian Captivity" stories emerged as a product of anti-Indigenous propaganda and were rife with stereotypes. Winnemucca counters these stereotypes in her own texts by providing instances of white colonial violence directed at the Piutes. She recounts "one of the Indians had a sister out digging some roots, and these white men went to the women who were digging, and caught this poor girl, and used her shamefully [...] it was on her account that her brother went and shot them" (Winnemucca 138). Her inclusion of this instance of abuse is strategic: it dispels the notion of white settlers as perpetual victims of Indigenous violence and contests the benevolence of colonial displacement. Winnemucca explains that the confrontation began when white men encroached on an Indigenous woman's space and raped her, subverting the reader's expectation of a captivity narrative where Indigenous men are instigators of brutality and violence against white settler women. The tropes typically applied to Indigenous captors are applied to white settler men in Winnemucca's text. Kleist references Gary Ebersole's work on "Indian captivity" narratives, in which he states the captive "undergoes various forms of degradation, as he is reduced to abject poverty, subjected to great physical deprivation, extreme hunger, and psychological stress, and divested of all status and power" (Kleist 80). The Piutes are "paid in clothes" rather than the one dollar per day they are initially promised (Winnemucca 213). They are starved, belittled, raped, and disempowered as a result of their displacement from the land, which was integral to their physical survival, and integral to the colonial project.

The clearest example of physical displacement as a site of pain is the forced march to the Yakima Reservation in the snow, during which many of the Piute succumb to illness or hypothermia, including Winnemucca's sister Mattie. Winnemucca describes her slow death at length: "Poor dear, she went on [...] She had great suffering during our journey" (Winnemucca 206); "All the time my poor dear little Mattie was dying little by little" (208); "Poor Mattie was so sick" (210); "On May 29, my poor little sister Mattie died. Oh, how she did suffer before she died! And I was left all alone" (Winnemucca 210). Her repetition of adjectives "poor", "little", and "dear" in relation to Mattie invokes sadness at her needless death. "Poor" suggests Mattie is deserving of pity and empathy, and "dear" and "little" suggest that she is cherished by the speaker. Winnemucca's emphasis on Mattie's suffering and her own subsequent loneliness contest the idea of displacement as leading to the betterment of Indigenous people. Winnemucca also juxtaposes life with death in close proximity on the forced march:

> We travelled all day [...] that night a woman became a mother; and during the night the baby died, and was put under the snow [... the mother] was almost dead when we went into camp. That night she too was gone, and left on the roadside, her poor body not even covered with the snow. In five days three more children were frozen to death, and another woman became a mother. Her child lived three days" (208)

The powerful imagery of the woman's body "left on the

roadside" in full view, and of the newborns dying reveals that colonial displacement spares no one, no matter how innocent. These passages work to invoke *pathos*, the third Aristotelian means of persuasion, which appeals to our emotional sensibilities as readers.

Winnemucca also includes numerous instances of sexual abuse in her memoir, including a father who searches for his missing children and finds them "lying on a little bed with their mouths tied up with rags [...] When my people saw their condition, they at once killed both brothers and set fire to the house. Three days after the news was spread as usual. "The bloodthirsty savages had murdered two innocent, hardworking, industrious, kind-hearted settlers" (Winnemucca 70). Like the deaths of Mattie and the newborns, this passage invokes *pathos* by showing the children held in captivity and gagged for sexual abuse. Winnemucca juxtaposes this with the "news as usual", identifying the captors and rapists as "innocent" and "kindhearted" which Winnemucca and the reader know to be untrue. This untruth is "usual" according to Winnemucca: it occurs consistently. In this package, she systematically dismantles the *ethos* of the colonial project, for which the untruth is an essential part.

Unlike *Life Among The Piutes, Winona* is fictional and therefore unburdened by the concept of objective truth. However, the story reflects the reality and brutality of enslavement and displacement. The transatlantic slave trade is a series of inherent displacements: first, a physical displacement from the ancestral homeland in Africa, and an immediate and subsequent displacement from personhood and humanity. While it is difficult to claim that Winona and Judah exist "outside of" the institution of slavery, we should read their departure from the slavers as an act of bold resistance. It is not accidental that fleeing slavers, an act which shows no compromise or appeasement, is the fate Pauline Hopkins assigned to her central characters: nor is it an accident that this displacement leads to a sense of freedom and belonging in Seneca tribal land.

Hopkins' disdain for liberation strategies that compromise with the oppressor emerged in her "growing frustration with Booker T. Washington's accommodationism" (Patterson 446). Booker T. Washington came to be associated with the "uplift ideal," emphasizing self-help and physical segregation of the races as key to Black success. In the opening paragraph of *Winona*, Hopkins' narrator explains "the world stand aghast and try in vain to find the dividing line supposed to be a natural barrier between the whites and the dark-skinned race" (Hopkins Chapter 1). In its earliest moments, *Winona* establishes it will be a contestational text, dispelling the notion of inherent racial differences. Hopkins' inclusion of the word "supposed" suggests there is no certain epistemology, urging us to question whether the dividing line exists at all. The first adjective Hopkins applies to the community in *Winona* is "mixed." She challenges not only segregation but the concept of race itself. After *Winona*'s publication, Hopkins was fired from the Colored American Magazine because "her attitude was not conciliatory enough [...] For the colored man to-day to attempt to stand up to fight would be like a canary bird facing a bulldog, and an angry one at that" (Patterson 446).

Both the Seneca and the African-Americans in *Winona* are experiencing "a diaspora, the possibility of cultural and racial genocide, and pressures to assimilate" (Patterson 448). They are also disenfranchised and displaced. The narrator says of the community that "nor were all who wore the tribal dress Indians. Here and there a blue eye gleamed or a glint of gold in the long hair falling about the shoulders told of other nationalities who had linked their fortunes with the aborigines" (Hopkins Chapter 1). Hopkins' choice to describe miscegenation as a "linked fortune"—as circumstance with positive connotations—is in direct opposition to prevailing forms of thought which constructed miscegenation as "the worst of all possible evils" (Patterson 449).

Displacement also offers Winona and Judah an escape from European parochial constructs of race and blood quantum, and divestment from patrilineal understandings of family. Judah is adopted by White Eagle, who in turn is adopted by the Seneca. Colleen O'Brien suggests that being raised on a secluded island means Winona and Judah "are not exposed to the logic and mastery that defines African or Native American '''blood' as inferior" (39). Adoption necessitates displacement from the family, land, or ethnicity of origin. The first mention of blood quantum appears only when Bill Thomson is introduced. He asks Judah and Winona if "[they are] Indians" to which Judah nods, only for Thomson to mutter "not by a long sight [...] nothin' but nigger blood ever planted the wool on top of that boy's head" (Hopkins Chapter 1). It is no coincidence that Thomson, one of *Winona*'s central antagonists, is deeply invested in the idea of blood quantum as a deliverer of intrinsic racial characteristics. The idea of Christian divine rule employed by John Brown to challenge blood quantum, as he recounts learning the Holy Writ "he hath made of one blood all the nations of the earth" (Hopkins Chapter 11). The religious unity of the abolitionists serves to construct Thomson, and subsequently blood quantum, as the antithesis of Christianity. Winona expresses scorn and resentment at the concept of racial hierarchy to Warren later in the text, saying "better an Indian than a Negro? I do not blame you for your preference" (Hopkins Chapter 14).

Before his leap into the stream, Thomson's lips are described as "bloodless" (Hopkins Chapter 15). It is ironic that after the emphasis he places on blood quantum as an intrinsic quality, he is described as "bloodless." While this is literal, because his lips are drained of all colour, bloodless also carries denotations of "cold and unemotional" and "lacking in vitality." When coupled with his "unhuman and appalling" scream, Thomson appears subhuman, supporting the theory of gradual dehumanization Aime Cesaire presents in *Discourse On Colonialism*: "colonization [...] dehumanizes the most civilized man [...] colonial activity, colonial enterprise, colonial conquest, which is based on contempt for the native and justified by that contempt, inevitably tends to change him who undertakes it [..] the colonizer, who in order to ease his conscience gets into the habit of seeing the other man as an animal accustoms himself to treating him like an animal, and tends objectively to transform himself into an animal" (Cesaire 41). After Judah throws Thomson to his assumed death, "in [Judah's] face [shines] a glitter of the untamable torrid ferocity of his tribe" (Hopkins Chapter 15). The possessive pronoun "his" suggests belonging, and the absence of an adjective such as "adoptive tribe" or "surrogate tribe" suggests finality.

Colleen O'Brien suggests that communion with the land gives freedom to Judah and Winona, and that displacement offers them an opportunity to relate to the land and one another in new ways. Early in the text, the narrator explains "though Erie County urged the Indians farther West, and took up their reservations for white settlers [...] The free air of the land of the prairies was not polluted by the foul breath of slavery" (Hopkins Chapter 1). Indigenous people are displaced, and the air of the land remains free and uncompromised by enslavement only because the settlers' "thirst for power stopped short" (Chapter 1). The West is a place 'free' from slavery for Black people because the settlers were satiated by colonial conquest against Indigenous people, which further complicates the relationship between the two groups. As Winona and Judah are continually displaced, their relationship with the land shifts. After Winona escapes the plantation, "the woods [calm] her" because they remind her of her time spent with the Seneca, where she experienced "not a thought of racial or social barriers" (Chapter 11). For Winona, the woods signal a physical displacement from chattel slavery.

Sarah Winnemucca and Pauline Hopkins shared a goal of instigating social and political change, and both were subject to scrutiny by the white supremacist colonial enterprise. Both struggled to achieve legitimacy in the eyes of the white reader. Both *Winona* and *Life Among the Piutes* address the predicament of displacement, which is the root of the Piutes' suffering, and the key to respite for Winona and Judah. In examining the ways in which displacement is perpetrated, these texts urge readers to critically examine the constructs that keep Black and Indigenous people and voices perpetually displaced.

1. Sarah Winnemucca Hopkins and Pauline Hopkins, who author the central texts discussed in this essay, have the same surname. MLA in-text citations require the author's surname, so for clarity, I have referred to Pauline Hopkins as "Hopkins", and Sarah Winnemucca Hopkins as "Winnemucca," honouring the names under which they published these works.

2

On Tampons, the Archive, and the Menses Bildungsroman

IN TSITSI DANGAREMBGA'S NERVOUS CONDITIONS

Tambu's description of her first period is the heart of Tsitsi Dangarembga's *Nervous Conditions*. In this passage, Dangarembga lays her claim to a significant history of menses *bildungsroman* narratives. From the trailblazing "Marjorie May's Twelfth Birthday" to the familiar and controversial *Are You There, God? It's Me, Margaret*, period narratives have always privileged the global north, the white, and the wealthy. Tambu reuses rags and recounts her initiation into menses by her aunts and grandmothers, and the moment is saturated with moodiness and misery. Burton insists that archives "are always already stories" that inspire speech, and that discussing and challenging the speech is imperative to history as a discipline (Burton 20). Foucault argues that the aim of 'questioning' documents has historically been "the reconstitution of the past from which they emanate" (Foucault 6). Tambu's first period itself merits an explication of its "unities, totalities, series, relations" through which it becomes a story, and therefore an archive.

Foucault acknowledges the document as an archaeological artifact in and of itself, imbued with history. Tambu's exposition therefore necessitates an interdisciplinary approach to history: through a cultural study of her anecdotal testimony, the material conditions of her existence can be better understood. Tambu notes that "during [her] first vacation home, [her] mother gave her some old napkins of Rambanai's [...] and instructed [her] to keep the napkins and [herself] particularly clean at that time of the month" (Dangarembga 97). Dangarembga's highly deliberate use of euphemism in the phrase "time of the month" reveals a historical reality that governs Tambu's life. Dangarembga's repetitive use of alliteration, such "nasty and nauseating" and "morose and moody" further emphasizes this reality: menstruation is shameful and requires discretion (97). When Tambu fails to be discreet and Nyasha offers her tampons, Dangarembga uses hyperbole to tell us Tambu "[dies] of embarrassment" (97). The intensity of Tambu's reaction reflects the gravity of her circumstances. Tambu uses euphemism again to refer to her vagina after she examines the diagram on a tampon box, asking herself if "it really [looks] like that on the inside" (97). Tambu's initial use of napkins creates a unique place for her in the archive of the female *bildungsroman*. She does not mention a

Procter & Gamble or Kimberly-Clark, the prototypical sanitary belt, or even cellucotton. Her story is not intended to swaddle young girls in the comfort of consumer capitalism, and Dangarembga makes clear that Tambu is not even afforded the illusion of a choice. Her explanation of her "problem" is clear; "tampons [are] expensive" (97). The narrative occurs in 1968 when tampons had barely existed for a generation, and like all new and convenient technology, their increased use illuminated the distinction between educated women who could afford them and the women living in relative and abject poverty who could not. However, Tambu clarifies that not all educated women are inclined to use tampons. Maiguru, who has a master's degree, "[knows] that tampons [are] offensive, that nice girls [do] not use them" (97). Dangerambga's word choice here is critical: Maiguru does not have an opinion about tampons, but a knowledge of them. Maiguru possesses a truth, and Tambu gives us no reason to believe Maiguru's "knowledge" is not based on empiricism. "Offensive" has many denotations according to the Oxford English Dictionary, including: invoking resentment or annoyance; disgusting; repulsive; and, actively aggressive. Dangarembga's use of "knowing" and "offensive" indicate a larger cultural consensus about tampons that extends far beyond personal prejudice. According to Nyasha, the only factor that will please Maiguru enough to provide them with tampons is that they are not pregnant. In *Nervous Conditions*, both being pregnant and menstruating (not being pregnant) are offensive. Tambu exists in a dichotomized world of "nice girls" and girls who use tampons. Power creates knowledge, and knowledge engenders power. Questioning the document is imperative to understanding the realities of Tambu's life, and by extension, the way she is interpellated as a subject.

Tambu's entire storied archive is embodied in her descriptions of her period. Anecdotes, especially those of women in subsaharan Africa, are subjugated forms of knowledge and have concomitantly been excluded from prevailing forms of thought: the archive is no exception. Tambu describes being initiated into menses through "conferences with older cousins and younger aunts, and the questions of older aunts and grandmothers" (97). Tambu is part of a tradition where women usher other women into the rite of menstruation, in an era where the role of the initiator is being progressively overtaken by companies. It is Nyasha that offers Tambu tampons, indicating that Tambu's support systems are lateral as well as intergenerational. Tambu is fascinated by the tampon instructions and their "curvaceous-line drawings [...] because [she has] not studied human reproduction at school" (97). Curricula have always held a critical place in the archive, especially when didactic. Does the diagram on the tampon box exist because of the massive disparities in education? We can deduce that evidence-based sex education was not afforded to anyone in 1968, and especially not to Africans at mission school, who Christian settlers saw as inherently sinful and licentious. The prospect of tampon use is anxiety-inducing for Tambu; she "[considers] aloud the consequences of pushing the offensively shaped object into [her] vagina" (97). This is the second time that Dangarembga uses "offensive" in relation to tampons, presumably due to their phallic shape. Nyasha proceeds to reassure Tambu that "[she is] better off losing [her] virginity to a tampon, which wouldn't gloat over its achievement, than to a man, who would add [hers] to his hoard of hymens" (97). The imagery of a "hoard of hymens" is furthered when Nyasha states "[men] wear them around their waists, like scalps" (97). Nyasha likening the possessiveness of male sexuality to scalping elicits another relevant archive. Scalping is historically and erroneously associated with Indigenous Africans as primeval, and the barbarity of the practice was used by settlers as evidence to justify colonial policies that left Africans largely impoverished and embittered. Dangarembga uses this simile to evoke the lingering damage of European Christian disinformation, which is ultimately the conclusion at which both Nyasha and Tambu arrive.

Tambu initially refers to her transfer to the mission school as the "period of [her] reincarnation" (94). Through treating Tambu's testimony as a piece of archival material, and reading the start of her menses through a Foucaultian lens, we are able to identify the historical power differentials that define the text. Like most archival material, Tambu's story takes a cross-section of society that reflects not only the zeitgeist but the material realities of an era.

3

"Where Youse Belong"

ON PLACEMAKING IN THE BLACK CANADIAN DIASPORA

Though Black Canadians people share a long history of curtailed belonging, our efforts to placemake in Canadian literary contexts look drastically different from other marginalized groups. Historically, Black definitions of belonging often use the European parochial metric of conquest. We strive to claim place, and by extension, identity, as we shape ourselves around what we call Canada, while also knowing that any claim to space or place here by settlers is only possible because of policies that violently empty the space of Indigenous people, both physically and conceptually.

To be Black in Canada is to be rendered invisible. In *Sometimes, A Motherless Child*, Austin Clarke uses repetitive foreshadowing and the conventions of Jamaican Patois to render anti-Black violence, and subsequently, Canadian Blackness, visible. Clarke's stark realism constructs a community that does the impossible and subverts anti-Blackness while also making it apparent.

In "Black W/Holes: A History of Brief Time", Marlene NourbeSe Philip posits that Blackness in Canada is always elsewhere and that through restrictions to our movement, we are forced to inhabit the "negative space" in Canada (Philip 120). We see the material ways in which Black lives are policed, and the ways in which this policing is rendered visible and resisted, in *Sometimes, A Motherless Child.*

Marlene NourbeSe Philip's hypothesis of Blackness is lived out in BJ's recollection of police brutality in his childhood. As BJ is forced into the police cruiser under a hail of profane, racist epithets, he hears "no, not in the fucking front seat, in the fucking back, where youse belong" (Clarke 360). This echoes Philip's sentiment: "you people will not be allowed to be all over this place called Canada. Except and in so far as we allow you to be" (Phillip 120). The plural "youse" indicates that the officer is not just addressing BJ, but all Jamaican men in the space called Canada. The use of "belong" reveals the conditionality of Canadian Blackness. Our belonging is constituted not by us, but by the white spaces which we inhabit and in which we are othered. BJ is not allowed to stand on the street unbothered. BJ is allowed to inhabit the back of the cruiser because his perceived inherent criminality under white supremacy dictates that is where he belongs. The back of the cruiser could easily be a placeholder for Philip's analysis of Caribana, as it is confined to the lakeshore and surveilled by helicopters. Wherever it is, the Black diaspora must be contained and closely observed, and its movement must be restricted. Clark's use of profanity and precise language makes this restriction visible and accessible to the reader.

Clarke consistently employs foreshadowing and precise diction to make the sociopolitical context of the text, and subsequently, Canada, clear to a presupposed white gaze. The first words BJ speaks aloud are "don't shoot, don't shoot" (Clarke 321). With this introduction, Clarke immediately places BJ's character in the cultural frame of police violence against black bodies. Shortly after, Clarke uses a third-person omniscient perspective to break the fourth wall as the unnamed mother thinks "here [is] another short story about Jamaicans and police" (341). This calls upon a shared cultural precedent to establish expectations for this story. The mother contemplates resisting by making a sign "in thick black letters: THIS COUNTRY RACIST. THE POLICE TOO!" (342). Clarke chooses to preface the words with the adjectives "thick" and "black", boldly and unapologetically making them visible and ensuring they take up physical space. Rather than write the words in lowercase and describe them as capitalized, Clark capitalizes on the page itself, rendering the words diegetically and extradiegetically visible and space-consuming. Anti-Black racism is no longer peripherized: it instead literally inhabits the "positive space" by virtue of being text, contrasting the whiteness relegated to the negative space of the page. The absence of the verb "is" between "country" and "racist" in these capitalized words reflects the structure of the mother's dialect of Jamaican Patois. In his refusal to place these critical words in the King's English, Clarke resists the expectation that Blackness must form itself around the Canadian dominant narrative. This forces a presupposed white reader to mold themselves around an unfamiliar dialect, subverting the power dynamics of Canadian anti-Blackness, while simultaneously bringing the same anti-Blackness to the forefront both within and outside of the text. Additionally, Clarke's omission of "is", a conjugation of the verb "to be," denies "THIS COUNTRY" of Canada its right to existence or state of being: the same right to existence and state of being that Canada routinely denies its Black people through systemic erasure and police violence. As the mother sits in the hair salon, an unnamed patron says "[she knows] a Jamaican man that the cops kill" (353). The use of the present infinitive tense, while reflecting Patois, also suggests that "the cops kill" this unidentified Jamaican man presently and in perpetuity. The unnamed man is always known by the unnamed woman, and he is always killed by the police. This once again underscores the likelihood that BJ will die before the story commences, but also makes apparent the continuous, uninterrupted nature of Canadian anti-Blackness.

The aftermath of BJ's death is also foreshadowed in Clarke's precise use of language. When BJ and Marco are pulled over and harassed, Clarke's narrator tells us "the policeman [seems] to see red" (351). The phrase 'seeing red' derives from the toreador's use of a red cape to agitate his bull, and paints the police officer as a deadly animal whose driving impetus is baseless rage. The narrator immediately amends this, and the succeeding sentence tells us "the policeman [seems] to feel his life [is] being threatened" (351). The sharp transition from a metaphor that centers the officer's uncontrolled anger, to careful and deliberate wording that emphasizes the danger to the officer's life, parodies the statements that follow police shootings of unarmed black men to justify the use of deadly force. In addition to foreshadowing BJ's death by deadly force, the change in wording transforms the policeman from the threat to the person being threatened. By positioning these vastly dissimilar sentences next to one another, Clarke allows us to see the process of how language simultaneously erases the reality of police violence and constructs the myth of threatening Blackness. In the initial pages of the text, it is clear what awaits BJ, but Clarke forces the reader to bear witness to the undeniable anti-Black violence that characterizes his life until the very end.

Perhaps the greatest distinction in Black diasporic writing is the imagining of an extradiegetic community in which we are seen and believed, and that has the subversive power to affect real-world change.

4

On Contact Zones, Safe Houses, and the Ahmed Mohamed Clock Incident

On September 14, 2015, fourteen-year-old Ahmed Mohamed brought a homemade clock to MacArthur High School in Irving, Texas, and was arrested and suspended after the school's administration believed his invention was a bomb (Kazi). Using an interdisciplinary approach, I will deconstruct primary source news articles and other cultural modes of production surrounding the Ahmed Mohamed Clock Incident.

In her keynote address to the Modern Language Association in 1991, Mary Louise Pratt introduced the concept of the "contact zone," which she defined as: "social spaces where cultures meet, clash, and grapple with each other, often in contexts of highly asymmetrical relations of power, such as colonialism, slavery, or their aftermaths as they are lived out in many parts of the world today" (Pratt 34). Pratt also puts forth the ideas of classrooms as "safe houses": "social and intellectual spaces where groups can constitute themselves as horizontal, homogenous, sovereign communities with high degrees of trust, shared understandings, temporary protections from legacies of oppression" (40). In her description of "safe houses," which exist separate from the contact zone, Pratt provides an example of a student asked to imagine an invention that will help their community; naturally, there is no better framework in which to situate the events of the Ahmed Mohamed clock incident of 2015. Studying primary source material surrounding the incident and its aftermath can provide insight into the power dynamics of the "contact zone" that emerged during and after the events at MacArthur High School, and of the implications this incident has for American society post-9/11.

The media sources following the Ahmed Mohamed clock incident are both primary sources and secondary sources, as they report on the event while also containing opinions and commentary. I acknowledge this, while contesting the notion of objectivity in journalism. Journalists are people, and people are susceptible to bias. I will examine where the reporting of the incident intersects with Islamophobic myth-making in the post-9/11 United States. This will allow for critical exploration of not only the events surrounding Ahmed Mohamed, but of 9/11 in historical perspective.

Following initial coverage of the incident in the *Dallas Morning News*, Mohamed was met with an outpouring of support from prominent figures such as Chris Hadfield, Mark Zuckerberg, and Barack Obama, with sympathetic columns in the *Huffington Post* and the *Los Angeles Times*. However, his story was instantly met with skepticism in other media sources. Several instances of media coverage attempt to portray Ahmed and his supporters as duplicitous and suspect, echoing the positioning of the East as the intrinsically untrustworthy "other" as addressed by Edward Said in *Orientalism*. These pieces use anecdotal evidence and unsubstantiated claims to construct MacArthur High School, and subsequently, American society, as a conceptual "safe house" rather than as a contact zone—one where power disparities reached their apex on September 14, 2015.

In "Ahmed Mohamed and the Imperial Necessity of Islamophilia," scholar Nazia Kazi explicitly argues that the Ahmed Mohamed clock incident "could be understood as forms of post-9/11 U.S. Islamophobia, and rightfully so," while also noting that Orientalism, racism, and xenophobia were likely factors. Kazi also addresses "Islamophilia"—the construct of the 'Good Muslim"—in relation to the incident. This aligns with Evelyn Alsultany's research on Islamophobic tropes that emerged in film and television post 9/11. Alsultany describes the "unusually sympathetic" character of the "Arab American as the unjust victim of post-9/11 discrimination" (Alsultany 161). Organizations such as the White House and Facebook tried to construct conceptual "safe houses" for Ahmed, but unlike previous media portrayals, sympathetic journalists acknowledged Ahmed's experience with the contact zone, rather than dismissing its existence altogether. Kazi uses this framework to characterize the positive treatment Mohamed received via social media, and criticizes White House's support following the incident, while Islamophobic policies remained in place.

CBS Dallas published an authorless story from a Muslim alumna of MacArthur High School stating that she had never experienced racism there, titled "Fellow Muslim Student Defends 'Clock Kid's' Former High School." In spite of what its title suggests, the article explicitly notes that the student refused to comment on Mohamed's experience, only saying that her own memory of her time there was positive when she had graduated years earlier. This is one of many articles that attempts to position the school as a "social and intellectual space where groups can constitute themselves as horizontal, homogenous sovereign communities with high degrees of trust [... and] temporary protections from legacies of oppression": as a "safe house."

Wall Street Journal editor James Taranto wrote in support of Ahmed's scientific pursuits, but declared that Islamophobia was a "pernicious myth," and that Ahmed simply faced similar treatment to "many Americans". In the *New York Post*, Kyle Smith echoed Taranto's sentiments in an opinion piece, writing that "95 per cent of Americans would [believe the clock] kinda looked like a bomb," and that "the left has been desperate to find some evidence, any evidence, that Muslims in general are facing deep-seated discrimination because a few Muslims attacked us on 9/11 [...] American Muslims have instead mostly been treated with respect and courtesy." Smith's characterization of the Muslim-American experience as one with mostly respectful and courteous encounters aligns with Mary Louise Pratt's "safe house." Both personal anecdotes and FBI statistics, which show a 1600% rise in Islamophobic hate crimes following 9/11, contest these statements (Alsultany 161). Both acts of violence by individuals and large-scale policy changes were noticed following 9/11. Evelyn Alsultany writes that "in just the first weeks and months after 9/11, the Council on American-Islamic Relations, the American-Arab Anti-Discrimination Committee, and other organizations documented hundreds of violent incidents experienced by Arab and Muslim Americans and people mistaken for Arabs or Muslims, including several murders [...] hundreds of Arab and Muslim Americans reported discrimination at work, receiving hate mail, and physical assaults, and their property, mosques, and community centers vandalized or set on fire [...] in the decade after 9/11, such discriminatory acts have persisted" (Alsultany 161). Alsultany also cites institutional examples of discrimination, such as the *USA PATRIOT Act*, the invasion of Iraq and Afghanistan, and the propagandizing of war (Alsultany 162). These characteristics are far more reminiscent of a contact zone, in which "cultures meet, clash, and grapple with each other, often in contexts of highly asymmetrical relations of power, such as colonialism, slavery, or their aftermaths as they are lived out in many parts of the world today," than they are reminiscent of a "safe house."

These statistics would not only contest Smith's notion that Islamophobia is a desperate search for "any evidence," but support the notion of Islamophobia as a rigorous existing body of interdisciplinary scholarship. Moreover, Smith's article is titled "How Ahmed's Clock Became a False, Convenient Tale of Racism." Before the article even begins, Mohamed's perspective and subsequently, racism are immediately designated "false." Like Taranto, Smith provides no research evidence for his claim that "95 percent of Americans" would also have reported and arrested Mohamed. None of his claims are substantiated beyond anecdotes and whataboutery, with statements such as "when is America going to get serious about the problem of white kids getting suspended from school for nothing?" In the first moments of the article, Smith describes Mohamed's invention as "a beeping, strange-looking homemade concealed device that turned out to be a clock," rather than as a clock that was mistaken for an explosive, which would be a more objective and accurate way of framing the events. The adjectives Smith assigns such as "strange-looking," "concealed," and "false," are subjective opinions, which is why the article must be examined as both a primary and secondary source. These adjectives also elicit notions of hidden motives, foreignness, and deceit: this is typical of the Orientalism that scholar Nazia Kazi argues is a factor in this incident, which will be explored later in this essay. Smith and Taranto fundamentally argue that Ahmed Mohamed was afforded equal treatment to other Americans: in other words, that the incident occurred in a conceptual "safe house." However, Smith also acknowledges that "even after the confusion [about the clock] passed, the boy was suspended from school" and that "police overreacted." If we are to combine his assertion that the police overreacted with his supposition that "95 percent of Americans" would have reacted exactly the same way, we are left with a culture in which "95 percent of Americans" overreact and suspend Muslim students without cause. These conditions resemble Pratt's contact zone—where "cultures meet, clash, and grapple with each other, often in contexts of highly asymmetrical relations of power, such as colonialism, slavery, or their aftermaths as they are lived out in many parts of the world today"—far more than they resemble the conceptual "safe house." In the context of these articles, journalists Smith and Taranto are critical and suspicious of a fourteen-year-old boy. Though they vehemently deny the existence of Islamophobia, the criticism itself has Islamophobic and Orientalist undertones. The power disparities and conflict represented by the article itself are also indicative of a contact zone in the aftermath of 9/11, rather than an egalitarian "safe house."

When applying Mary Louise Pratt's theoretical framework to the Ahmed Mohamed Clock Incident, it would appear that MacArthur High School and the world of journalism continue to be "contact zones" and not "safe houses:" however, instead of Pratt's examples of slavery and colonialism, this contact zone exists in the aftermath of 9/11, and of the invasion of Iraq and Afghanistan. The media coverage of this MacArthur High School indicates that the incident may be a microcosm for the post-9/11 political climate in America, if, as Taranto suggested, "many Americans" experience what Ahmed Mohamed did on September 14, 2015: and if, as Smith suggested "95 percent of Americans" would choose to enact it on him.

5

On "Brokeback Mountain"

QUEERNESS, SETTLEMENT, AND MASCULINITY IN THE AMERICAN WEST

Annie Proulx's short story "Brokeback Mountain" holds a contested status as a Western narrative. Its portrayal of queer cowboys is perceived by some as a "perverted mockery of the western" and subsequently, as an attack on the American mythos of the west (Needham 33). This suggests that when queer perspectives are introduced, the narrative of the West as we know it begins to disintegrate. Brokeback Mountain complicates our notions of settlement and masculinity. By examining the ways in which Jack and Ennis conform to and resist the settler masculine ideal, we begin to see the limits of the frontier and of the West.

The nomadic lifestyle of Jack and Ennis in Brokeback Mountain forces us to reexamine our problematic definitions of "settled." While there is no singular standard for what constitutes a settlement, Limerick introduces us to Harold Simonson's notation that an area of the West was considered by some scholars to be settled when two persons inhabited a square mile, because this signified the end of the frontier (23). Simonson's definition does not include stipulations about time spent living on the land, or the relationship between the two persons, or the relationship between the land and its inhabitants. Should the land be configured from matter to property? Should the relationship be symbiotic, or must it only benefit the settler? By Simonson's metric, Ennis and Jack are settled in their tent on Brokeback Mountain. However, this definition presents inherent issues. It relies on a presupposition that, prior to the two persons arriving, the land is empty. It says nothing about the Indigenous people who have inhabited the West since time immemorial, but who are never afforded the title of settlement. Simonson's definition erases the Westward expansion of the United States that allows Brokeback Mountain and other constructs of the frontier to exist on land that is notably entirely absent of women and Indigenous people. The events on Brokeback Mountain are made possible by settler colonial policy, which violently emptied the land of its original inhabitants.

While the scholars to whom Simonson refers may or may not have accepted Jack Twist and Ennis del Mar's encampment as "settled", their queerness further complicates this categorization. While "settled" retains its colonial definition, it also refers to "[adopting] a more steady or secure style of life, especially in a permanent job and home" (OED). It is difficult to define a queer couple "settling" when the goals of homeownership, employment, family are not only heteronormative but practically inaccessible. Ennis and Jack do not find permanent work, permanent homes, or permanent families: Ennis and Alma get divorced, and Jack is an absent husband and father. Rather than "settle" with one another, Ennis and Jack choose to "settle": that is, they "accept or agree to something that one considers to be less than satisfactory" (OED). Ennis is compelled by fear to acquiesce to a "failed heteronormative existence", and Jack is compelled by Ennis' refusal to "settle" with him. Though both men lay a sentimental and emotional claim to Brokeback Mountain, there is no physical permanency to their settlement. When Jack's ashes are not scattered there as per his dying wish, the narrative denies the men all permanent settlement at Brokeback Mountain. The closing of the frontier is withheld from them as queer men.

Jack and Ennis consistently try and fail to achieve legitimacy in settler-colonial terms. Limerick identifies the frontier as the focal point of conquest, where "the pursuit of legitimacy in property overlapped with the pursuit of legitimacy in way of life and point of view" (Limerick 27). Their plight appears to support Jack Halberstam's framework of queerness as a series of failures. Halberstam writes that "queerness offers the promise of failure as a way of life [...] but it is up to us whether we choose to make good on that promise in a way that makes a detour around the usual markers of accomplishment and satisfaction" (186). Ennis and Jack adhere to masculinity in a number of ways but deviate from it at its intersections with settler colonialism. Ennis marries Alma, has children, swears, gets violent, and drinks to excess; however, his most overt displays of traditional masculinity typically follow instances of being outed. When Alma confronts Ennis about his fishing trips with Jack, declaring "[she knows] what it means", Ennis "[seizes] her wrist", causing her to break a dish (Proulx 26). He negates Alma's "I know" by responding "you don't know nothin" (] 26). Alma's knowledge of the affair could endanger Ennis, but the finality of his assertion combined with his violence allows him to retain power. His epistemology is absolute, and he forces Alma to accept it by threatening to make her and Bill "eat the fuckin floor" (27). He "[gets] drunk, [has] a short dirty fight" as he tries and fails to enact the domination required of him as a settler man (27).

If the pursuit of legitimacy in property overlaps with the pursuit of legitimacy in way of life as Limerick suggests, Ennis and Jack are consistently illegitimate. Ennis opts to "[stay] in the little apartment" with Alma in Riverton, "which he [favours] because it [can] be left at any time" (Proulx 17). If we are to view the West as a focal point of conquest, Ennis fails the requisite conquering of vast expanses of land. He rejects the permanency of settlement in favour of nomadism, subverting our expectations of a Western protagonist, while simultaneously ensuring there will be no definite end to the frontier. His failure as a breadwinner leads Alma to deny him the success of having more children, stating "I'd have 'em if you'd support 'em" (25). Her marriage to the Riverton grocer who employs her solidifies Ennis's failure. Even on the revered Brokeback Mountain, Ennis and Jack fail in their role as shepherds. When Ennis spends an entire night with Jack in the main camp, "the sheep [take] off west and [get] among a herd in another allotment" (Proulx 14). The sheep taking off "west" in the blowy hailstorm is critical: as Proulx provides no specificity about the sheep's whereabouts beyond "west", this sets up Jack and Ennis in juxtaposition to the ambiguous "West". The pathetic fallacy is clear: Ennis and Jack disrupt the narrative of the West by settling with one another — a phenomenon as out of place as a hailstorm in August. The hailstorm disrupts the land, sheep, and jeopardizes their livelihood. The sheep are lost for five days total, and when they return Ennis knows they are "mixed", and notes that "everything [seems] mixed" (14). Like Ennis and Jack, the sheep travel "west", and return profoundly and irreparably different. This constructs Brokeback Mountain as a land of liminality and opportunity.

Ennis and Jack's relationship does not fulfill traditional markers of accomplishment and satisfaction, and as Halberstam suggests, fulfills the promise of failure. Their relationship does not progress by any heteronormative metrics: marriage, children, prolonged cohabitation, or even sexual exclusivity. When Jack reflects on their twenty-year courtship, he says that "all [they] have is Brokeback Mountain" (Proulx 33). In the literal sense, they never "have" or possess Brokeback Mountain in settler-colonial terms because the land never makes the transition from matter to property. Brokeback Mountain offers a temporal space where they can cohabitate, and cultivate sexual exclusivity and intimacy. Paradoxically, because of the settler-colonial displacement of Indigenous people that constructs the West, Jack and Ennis are offered a brief recess from the demands of settler-colonial manhood. Ennis and Jack's final argument is succeeded by the narration "nothing ended, nothing begun, nothing resolved" (Proulx 33). Ennis and Jack's affair on Brokeback Mountain could be read as a microcosm for the frontier, as a place of continuity which, as Limerick argues, has no definite beginning, end, or resolution. Because they never inhabited the encampment together again, by Simonson's definition, the frontier was never closed.

Technology may help us better understand "Brokeback Mountain" and its adherence to — and deviation from - the Western. Limerick tells us that historians are at an impasse about narratives that unfold in the latter half of the twentieth century being categorized as Westerns. "Brokeback Mountain" contains the mules, sheep, and bulls one would expect from a Western alongside the modernity of pickup trucks. Technology as a deciding factor is a "judgment of sentiment and nostalgia—in favor of tools controllable by one person, and supposedly closer to nature, and against the intrusion of modern machinery" (Limerick 24). Both men assume the ancient, mythologized role of shepherd, which places the narrative perceptibly closer to the land and to nature. The criteria Limerick introduces supports the phallocentrism of the time spent on Brokeback Mountain. The sex between Jack and Ennis share involves Ennis' penis, which is controlled by him. He explains there is "no instruction manual needed", signifying the naturality of the act (Proulx 13). The concludes when Ennis exclaims "gun's goin off", aligning his penis with the famed symbol of Western myth, and finalizing that no modern machinery is needed to facilitate the sex. Ennis and Jack's coupling lacks the requisite sentiment and nostalgia of the Western because queer narratives are entirely absent from the genre. In this sense, "Brokeback Mountain" constructs a new memory of the West, which accounts for a multiplicity of lived experiences.

The tire iron is perhaps the most nuanced piece of technology in the narrative. In itself, it is just a warped piece of steel to be operated manually. It is unsophisticated and practical, and loosely adheres to the criteria Limerick addresses, but the symbolism it accrues in the story makes it much more nuanced. For Ennis, the tire iron is the quintessence of the violent homophobia around which his life is shaped. It is an instrument of the modernity he vehemently resists, and a sign of the finality of time which he greatly fears. It is fitting that the violent explosion of a tire caused by a damaged bead, or the violent use of a tire iron caused by a damaged more, would be the cause of Jack's demise. Whether Jack is killed by the tire iron or not is immaterial: it only matters that Ennis believes he was. The encampment on Brokeback Mountain was a refuge from modernity, and the tire iron disrupts this refuge. Ennis recounts Jack eating from a can with a spoon and notes "the spoon handle [is] the kind that [can] be used as a tire iron" (40). The imagery of the tire iron intrudes on his most cherished memories of Jack, and it becomes the antithesis to the fearless time spent on Brokeback Mountain.

In this short story, Annie Proulx reveals the homoeroticism of the American frontier and of the quintessential cowboy. Gary Needham posits that queering a genre involves making it oblique, and Proulx does this by introducing the reader to alternate ways of being in the West. Ennis and Jack struggle and fail to conform to settler-colonial standards of masculinity, and in doing so, cultivate perhaps the most intense and tragic love story present in a Western (Needham 33).

6

On Queer Shame And Serophobia in Fight Club

It is October 15, 1999. George Michael's "Praying for Time" tops the charts, people living with HIV or AIDS will be barred from entering the United States for eleven more years, and David Fincher's *Fight Club* is premiering in theatres across the country. Tyler Durden spits blood in the face of Lou five years after AIDS is declared the leading cause of death for all Americans aged twenty-five to forty-four. Six months after Lou lets Tyler use the basement, President Bill Clinton declares AIDS a threat to national security. *Fight Club*, like all film, can—and should—be examined as archival material. It takes a cross section of queer society, and accurately captures the serophobic zeitgeist of the end of the millennia. It "[produces] and [incorporates] ideologies that represent the outcome of struggles marked by the historical realities of power and the deep anxieties of the times" (Giroux 687).

At the beginning of the epidemic, a New York Times article dubbed the virus 'GRID' (Gay-Related Immunodeficiency). From its first moments in the public sphere, AIDS is inextricably linked with queerness. Stigma against persons living with HIV and AIDS (PHAs) is pervasive because HIV is the illness most associated in the public conscience with queer folk. Homophobia exacerbates serophobia and vice versa: the dynamics of this socio-political entanglement are in action when Tyler interacts with Lou. When Lou first enters the basement, Tyler asks him who he is, to which Lou responds:

> Who am I? There's a sign on the front that says 'Lou's Tavern'. I'm fucking Lou. Who the fuck are you? [...] Who told you motherfuckers that you could use my place? Irving? Irving's at home with a broken collarbone. You don't own this place. I do. [...] Look, stupid fuck. I want everybody out of here right now. [...] Did you hear what I just said? (Fincher 01:11:19 - 01:12:57)

Lou is immediately assertive and does not hesitate to remind Tyler repeatedly that *he* owns the space with repeated use of "my" and first-person pronouns. Lou proceeds to beat a limp and disengaged Tyler, who laughs. When Lou walks away, Tyler immediately jumps on top of him, coughing and spitting blood into his face, shouting "you don't know where I've been, Lou, you don't know where I've been" (01:13:44). Lou sobs "Oh God, God, fucking use the basement, Christ"

(01:13:55). Serophobia is deployed as power here as Lou acquiesces to Tyler's demands. Tyler is deliberately evoking Lou's presumed homophobia, and concomitantly, his serophobia. The phrase "you don't know where I've been" carries connotations of disease when applied to animals. Tyler does not say "I may have HIV" because he does not have to; the mere allusion combined with the overt homoeroticism of Fight Club is enough. By refusing to disclose more specifically, a folkway always demanded of PHAs, Tyler resists legibility.

No illness is considered more of a personal failing than HIV because of its association with queerness, a capital failure in a heteronormative society. This conflation is so pronounced that it denies heterosexual PHAs opportunities and livable lives (as was the case with Ryan White), and it denies queer folk who are HIV-negative opportunities and livable lives (as is the case with blood bans and discriminatory hiring practices). When Tyler weaponizes this stigma to gain an opportunity, he introduces an alternate way of being. He enacts this subversive failure because he "recognizes that alternatives are embedded already in the dominant and that power is never total or consistent" (Halberstam 108). He "[refuses] to acquiesce to the dominant logics of power and discipline" (109).

It is October 15, 1999, a year and nine days after Matthew Shepard's beating death in Fort Collins, Colorado. It will be ten years before Congress passes the *Matthew Shepard and James Byrd Jr. Hate Crimes Prevention Act*, adding a victim's actual or perceived sexual and gender identity to existing hate crime criteria. On October 15, 1999, being queer is deadly, and this deadliness is materialized in the character of Robert Paulson.

We are first introduced to Robert Paulson through the knowledge that he is intersex:

> Bob. Bob had bitch tits. This was a support group for men with testicular cancer. The big moosie slobbering all over me? That was Bob. [...] Eight months ago Bob's testicles were removed. Then hormone therapy. He developed bitch tits because his testosterone was so high and his body upped the estrogen. And that was where I fit. (00:03:10 - 00:03:42)

The diction the narrator uses is significant as he describes "fit[ting]" in Bob's breasts. Here, he iterates that he has discovered a new sense of belonging and a new way of being in Robert Paulson's intersex body. When the narrator first interacts with Bob, he notices "his eyes [are] already shrink-wrapped in tears": he also notes his "knees [are] together" and he takes "awkward little steps" (00:07:40- 00:08:10). The only characteristics of Bob that the narrator vocalizes are ones that pertain to his intersex body, and in this, Bob is perpetually constituted by his failure.

Even before his cancer, Robert Paulson desperately tries to quantify and make tangible his masculinity. His bankruptcy, divorce, and estrangement from his children means he is failing in a heteronormative, capitalist society, which equates success "to specific forms of reproductive maturity combined with wealth accumulation" (Halberstam 15). He and the narrator repeat the group's slogan: "We're still men, yes, we're men, men is what we are" (Fincher

00:03:20-00:03:30). Their use of this slogan is necessitated by Bob's hyperawareness of his own failure, and the narrator's fixation on Bob's failure as a source of relief and enlightenment. With his face in Bob's breasts, the narrator's inner monologue makes a sharp transition: "And then it happened. I let go, lost in oblivion, dark and silent and complete. I found freedom. Losing all hope was freedom" (00:09:00 - 00:09:25). Here, the narrator describes discovering alternate ways of being and knowing that arise from literally and figuratively embracing the most noticeable parts of Bob's failure - his "bitch tits".

Robert Paulson is murdered by the police after a stint of direct action. He and other members of Project Mayhem "destroy a piece of corporate art and trash a franchise coffee bar" (01:45:30-01:45:45). Bob fails to escape a police pursuit and is shot in the head. Bob's existence is defined by "emptiness, futility, limitation, ineffectiveness, sterility, unproductiveness" (Halberstalm 131). Although Robert Paulson's murder is not a positive aspect of failure, it illustrates the material, real-life consequences of failing in a heteronormative capitalist society. Bob exists outside of the heterosexual binary, and his life is designated as unimportant and unliveable. Robert Paulson's murder makes hegemony visible. He is murdered because he is a man with breasts and a high voice; a man who cries and hugs other men; a man who fails repeatedly and spectacularly at heteronormativity and cisnormativity. This failure is punishable by violent, public death and any chance he has at a livable life is erased.

Fight Club encompasses many ways of being queer, and

many ways of failing. Project Mayhem is a collective of men who shed all material possessions and cohabit in a ramshackle house while explicitly saying that they do not need women. Fight club is conceived because men are urgently seeking alternate ways of being and knowing. The non-linear structure of the film disrupts the discipline of time and provides us with a new way of understanding the events. Most significantly, *Fight Club* illustrates what queer folk have always known: that stigma has a material existence and that it is constituted in every interaction a queer person has. These interactions can be subversive, as in the case of Tyler and Lou, or silencing and sobering, as in the case of Robert Paulson. *Fight Club* encompasses queer experiences of belonging and unbelonging, of legibility and illegibility. It is truly a cross-section of queer life.

creative nonfiction

7

On Intersectionality

This is a piece I wrote and delivered at Slutwalk Guelph, on a cold, bitter morning in April of 2018.

CW: Sexual assault, antiblackness, queerphobia, Islamophobia

Last summer I was in Church and Wellesley Village,
standing at the intersection of
    racialized sexism
    and
    sexualized racism.
I wore some killer high heels
and a nylon skirt that said
    "Barbie"
and life in plastic was fantastic
until I heard some men on the corner yell that they wanted to
    touch my hair and
    undress me everywhere.
I ran the permutations and
took advantage of the broad daylight and

the thirty feet of space between us.
>I flipped the bird,
yelled some angry words
>and brushed their cruelty off my shoulders.
The man I was with, a Well-Intentioned Ally, was standing.
Watching.
Silent.
Later he would see me doing the same,
and say of the scene
>"Well, I couldn't intervene."
>"What if they had a gun?"
he says of those
>young
>Black
>men
in the summer sun.
What do I say now?
Black says
>"Do not assume every one of us you see on the corner
>is itching for your blood"
White feminism says
>they were misogynists, and violence stays on misogyny like white on ICE
Expectations say
>"why couldn't you stand up for me?" And
womanism says, "I am tired."
>A man that knew I what had I survived,
>knew I struggled to flourish and thrive, and

he couldn't leverage his privilege once
He couldn't put my safety before his comfort
> But I'm always standing at that intersection.

What can I say when the cop who speaks out about sexual harassment in the workplace is the same one who screamed
"ALL LIVES MATTER"
in my sister's face
while she minded her business
at work one day?
What can I say when the high school guidance counsellor
who is the pillar for queer allyship,
tells me to Forgive the Boy
who wanted to immolate me because I was Muslim?
That he was brilliant
and it was me who didn't understand
his sense of humour?
What can I say when my fellow East African girl,
a beacon of black liberation,
says people like me
belong in conversion therapy?
> We must amend the way we talk about pain.

The perimeter of pain is not a white picket fence,
> or a gated community,
> or schoolyard chain link,
> or even barbed wire.

The perimeter of pain is the monopoly that we create when we speak about it
> with country club exclusivity,
> where the only way women like me can get in
> is if we're cutting trees,

if we are a caddy on the course of our own conversations.

We must redefine the word Survivor.

Survivor is the hero with a thousand beat faces.
Survivor wears a hijab
and hennaed hands
and they tell her that her memory is failing
Survivor wears beauty supply store hoop earrings
and a 30-inch Brazilian weave with silk lace closure
and she hasn't felt clean since she was twelve years old
Survivor wears a Chanel no. five o' clock shadow
and the pain of alienation from her own body and bathroom
Survivors are the heroes with a thousand beat faces,
and victim-blaming
and body policing
have just as many masks.

And it is everyone's obligation to intervene when so many of us are frozen at intersections.

Why did the survivor cross the road?
She didn't
They stopped her at the intersection.

8

On University Librarians

il·lu·mi·nate
/iˈlo?omə,nāt/
verb

1. *make (something) visible* or bright by shining light on it; light up.
2. *help to clarify* or explain.
3. decorate (a page or letter in a manuscript) by hand with gold, silver, or colored designs.

The first time I thumbed through an illuminated medieval manuscript, my Special Collections librarian Melissa McAfee cautioned me not to touch the text itself. It was printed on vellum made from unborn calf skin, which made the gold-embellished pages slippery and the lettering vulnerable to the oils on my fingertips. I was a fumbling, anxious third-year student, holding a Vulgate Bible that predated the printing press. These manuscripts were on loan to our library from Chicago, and it was my job as a student assistant to prepare them for their debut in our exhibit room. I nestled them into acid-free book cradles that would support their fragile spines, and held open their delicate pages with "book snakes"—weighted strings used for precious materials. These manuscripts would sit in the same glass display cases that I admired for hours on the day I first entered the library.

Between Romanesque halls and residences on the University of Guelph's central campus stands a six-storey Brutalist building with a stern but kind face. Floor-to-ceiling windows swaddle its entrance, inviting enough light to illuminate the building, but not weather the books. Shelves holding free resources, citation guides, and writing-help sheets flank the soft, worn pleather armchairs on the first floor. Colourful wall decals wind around concrete pillars and climb to the ceiling like vines, chanting the phrase "This is your library." Past the Starbucks line that twists around the first floor, a giant U-shaped desk sits emblazoned with the words "ASK US." This is where your library journey begins.

The first thing you must know before entering is that every librarian is a superhero: one you deserve *and* one you need right now. Librarians teach you to find reliable and credible academic sources. They help you find peer-reviewed sources for your papers, perfect your bibliography, and connect you with faculty. They illuminate the dark jungle of post-secondary education. In the first week of my first year, a professor tasked our class with finding a physical copy of

Plato's *Republic*, and made us photograph ourselves with the book as proof. I resented this paternalistic request until I realized it was his way of getting us acquainted with our library. Within one minute of conversing with a librarian, I'd learned which floor, hallway, and shelf the book was on. I've never forgotten that day.

Working in my library has allowed me to see the magic unfold behind the scenes. I work in the archives under Melissa's mentorship, scanning and digitizing material to meet professional librarian standards. I have seen the worn grout on our cultural mosaic: scribbled notes from Order of Canada members; Anishinaabeg community cookbooks; memoirs of a London, Ont., artist and ex-seminarian who fell victim to the HIV epidemic. I have laughed at my desk late at night at a decades-old resumé from a seventh-grade boy auditioning for a musical at London's Grand Theatre written entirely in Comic Sans font and embellished with stickers. I wept with joy for him when I found his name on a house program, with the fluorescence and monotonous sound of the scanner humming beside me.

I wanted to be a mouthpiece for stories I read in the archives. With Melissa's support, I published my own book illuminating anti-Blackness in Canadian food history. Its pages contain minstrel advertisements and mammy caricatures pulled from Canadian cookbooks in our own archives. Melissa mentored me on how to safely and mindfully digitize images from books that were a century old. She introduced me to Ali Versluis, our Open Education Librarian, who taught me about copyright so that I could license my own work. After its publication with the Guelph Black Heritage Society, Melissa proudly displayed *The Cook Not (Even) Mad, Or, Womanist Cookery* on our website's front page, where it resides to this day. I realize now that she was my mouthpiece.

All librarians become mouthpieces. They make visible those who have been lost to time and advocate for those who struggle to find their voices now. I only hope that if I am lucky enough to become a librarian myself, I can supervise a nervous undergrad as she discovers the magic of illumination.

9

On Canada

This is a transcript of the short piece I shared at Lights for Liberty, a protest against migrant detention, in Waterloo Town Square on Friday July 12, 2019. I want to thank Joy Harris for suggesting my name to Healy Thompson, who helped organize this event.

I want to thank the organizers of Lights for Liberty for allowing me to speak here tonight. I am humbled by the words of our Indigenous leaders who are always at the forefront of struggles for social and environmental justice. For those of you who don't know me, I work in the archives, and my job largely consists of scanning and digitizing archival material to meet professional librarian standards. Every shift, a cross-section of society passes through my EPSON Expression 10000XL scanner.

The past many know is not the past I know.

The Canada many see is not the Canada I see.

I see fragments of a bitter past flicker by like stubborn stains that no amount of soda water can displace.

I see concepts of 'legal' and 'illegal', ever faltering but always trailing behind the prevailing form of thought, a Eurocentric, Americentric colonial mentality that privileges the global north and the bottom line.

I see a cultural mosaic.

I blink.

I see Indigenous accounts deliberately and maliciously excluded and erased by complicit settler historians and archivists.

I see censorship.

I see a diverse tapestry.

I blink.

I see the back of that tapestry and it is a goddamn mess.

I see hundreds of letters - Canadian ministers informing Black sharecroppers in the south that our soil cannot sustain fruit, corn or livestock to keep them out of the Great White North.

I see the sanitized dominant narrative.

I squint.

I see "none is too many".

I see Japanese Canadians in sugar beet shacks, detained and dispossessed.

I see the first recorded race riot in North America.

I see Calixa Lavallée, the composer of our national anthem, in minstrel after minstrel after blackface minstrel.

I see the St. Louis turned away from Pier 21 in Halifax, its figurehead a lead casket, its coffin regifted buoyancy.

I see babies ripped from mothers

and babies ripped from mothers
and babies ripped from mothers.

I see justice compound fracturing under our long and proud history of complicity.

We must divest from this legacy of doing nothing.

We must understand that the history we think is the objective truth is carefully curated, with more omitted than included.

As settlers, it is our obligation to act when we see our own dictating who can and cannot take up space on this land.

We must amplify the voices of marginalized people,
who have trailblazed resistance on this land.

We must abandon performative gestures for meaningful change and leverage our privilege.

We must acknowledge the history so we can effectively unite and mobilize against human detention.

Remember, justice carries a sword alongside her scales.

10

Critical Mass

ON BLACK ART IN WHITE SPACES

From September 13, 2018 to January 6, 2019, the Art Gallery of Guelph is hosting the distinctly Black exhibition, *Critical Mass*. Guelph is a city in which Black people fight tirelessly for the space to be seen and heard, and for the recognition to see and hear one another. Though we have inhabited this area since the Queen's Bush settlement of the early nineteenth century, our enduring presence is under constant threat of erasure. The institution of the art gallery, much like the city of Guelph, is a white space not because there are no Black artists, but because art has been fundamentally misunderstood to entail the occupation and domination of physical space. Galleries are first and foremost highly colonial institutions that often deal in stolen treasures, and they are part of a greater institution: one that deals in stolen land and stolen people. The word "art" is thought to necessitate some highly specialized discourse that has been largely inaccessible to Black folk. In a contextualization of their piece *Compromise*, the Black Artists Union states "as art being a language to connect with others," establishing that "this is a platform to help develop skills for navigating and engaging in art spaces".

Compromise is an explicitly and exclusively Black art space situated in the Judith Nasby Gallery. Upon entering the space, I am greeted with a vast expanse of white wall. A black mat surrounds white words, and I ponder the curatorial function of this choice. I think even with inverted colours, Blackness occupies the negative space: it is a seemingly shapeless mass acquiescing to accommodate the sharp lines and curves of whiteness. But the white words tell a Black story; one of compromise. Opposite this wall is a Black curtain separating *Compromise* from the rest of the exhibit. To the left of this curtain is another Black sign with white words.

"This is a Black only space. Please, if you are not Black, do not enter."

The words are clear and accessible even when typical colours are inverted, and they remain clear when power structures of segregation through signage are illuminated. It calls into question who is allowed to make signage. What does claiming space mean? Why does enacting a claim to space require more from us than it requires white folk? Why is existing in a space for centuries not enough? I contemplate the use of the word "please". I contemplate the historical implications of racialized signage. I think of Greensboro and of Johannesburg, of boiling hot coffee and of acid in swimming pools. I think of how Jim Crow never said "please" and how

UNDERGRAD | 61

Apartheid never said "please" because they did not have to. I think of how even in this context, in true Black Canadian fashion, we ensure our space is protected by being polite. Politeness works, sometimes.

Upon entering the space, I am instantly aware of the squeak of my sneakers, and so is Jared, a fellow Black student. He greets me with a smile. Later, he confesses that upon hearing my footsteps, he assumed that a non-Black person had disregarded the sign and invaded the space. He stands at the far end of the space, looking at *Misogynoir: This Ain't A Special Occurrence* by Toronto-based artist Jemini J. Baptiste. If the hallmark of good art is the invocation of emotion, this work succeeds. The piece bleeds exhaustion. I tell Jared the fragmented Instagram conversation matted on photos of dark-skinned Black women is familiar: he responds the most abused members of our communities are Black women. We echo Malcolm X and W.E.B. DuBois. We speak and move through space freely, none of our words or interactions presupposing a white gaze. Though I have failed to ascertain whether this was a curatorial goal, Jared and I now follow each other on Instagram. *Compromise* creates the space for camaraderie: it is the teacher's lounge of Black Canada, a temporary refuge from inappropriate questions where genuine connections can be forged and we can be unapologetically ourselves.

Compromise is a sensory and fully immersive experience. The space is intimate in a way that the larger exhibit is not. In the centre of the room is a rocking chair, a colourful quilt tossed casually over it. Fragrant sandalwood incense and ashes sit on a side table next to family photo albums. Curtia Nichole Wright's *Sunday* combines audio and video in an artful exploration of Black domesticity. In *Aunties, Mommy, and YUNGLUV*, Sydne Barnes Wright gives the average Black gallery patron unprecedented visibility. The notion that everyday images of Black individuals, Black couples, and Black families can and should occupy artistic space is embodied here. *Over Water*, an exploration-based PC video game by Zoma Tochi Maduekwe, allows me to engage with colour and movement in a new way and reminds me that video games are not always made for everyone. *Compromise* is alive and breathing. I am enveloped by colour and texture, by scent and by sound, and for the first time in my life, I see myself in art.

According to the label that accompanies *Compromise*, the Black Artists Union aims "to represent the ideas and work of contemporary Black creators". They meet this objective, and like archivists, their compiled work shows us a cross-section of Black Canada. The space combines past and present in a way that simultaneously acknowledges our hardships and celebrates our continued resilience. The question of what representation looks like in effect is answered by *Compromise* without tokenization or detraction. The Judith Nasby Gallery is Black and art is Black. Guelph is Black and Canada is Black.

11

"Keep The Volume Low"

ON BEING BLACK ON CAMPUS

vol·ume
/ˈvälyəm,ˈväl,yoʔom/
noun
a book forming part of a work or series.
the amount of space that a substance or object occupies, or that is enclosed within a container, *especially when great.*
quantity or *power of sound*; degree of loudness.

The Sign adorns a purple pillar in the Guelph Black Students Association room, formerly the C.J. Munford Centre, at the University of Guelph. It stands opposite to a whiteboard sporting a colour coded-map of the world. Dry erase tells the story of our members, who delineate their nations of origin in Africa and the Caribbean with bubble letters and smiley faces.

I love the GBSA room. I love that its microwave is so often spinning—sometimes with popcorn, sometimes last night's rice and peas. I love its "complimentary" family-sized bottle of St. Ives lotion (a bottle of "complimentary" hot sauce for the shared fridge is pending). I love its Art Deco upholstery, and how it so perfectly coheres with the room's purple accents. I love that all the usual signs that inhabit shared spaces—"please clean up your messes'"—are absent, because we treat the space with the same respect we would our mother's house. I love everything about the GBSA room, except that Sign.

It says:
Please remember to
Keep the volume low
To be mindful of our neighbours
THANKS!

"How long has that been there?" I asked when I first noticed it last January, addressing no one in particular.

"A few weeks. Someone complained."

The "please" and "thank you" are dwarfed: clearly an afterthought. I wonder if every other club on campus has a similar sign.

They don't.

In his memoir *In The Black: My Life*, radio giant and Guelph alumnus Brandeis Denham Jolly writes that in 1954, the University of Guelph was 10 percent Black—"as integrated as Canada got at that time." Students from the West Indies came here to study agriculture and be caricatured in the school's newspaper. A chaplain on campus counseled white girls not to date Black students. Minstrel shows were put on by the Ontario Agricultural College, which I've written about before. Jolly once watched a student drop a cigarette on the floor, and heard another respond "Don't worry—we'll get some n****r to clean it up."

I think of what 10 percent Black looks like. What would it be like to see one in ten people on campus who look like me? The school doesn't collect race-based data anymore, but anecdotally, it's far from 10 percent Black. On a lucky day, I may see ten Black students, total. This room is my only reprieve, and I've catalogued its sweet cacophony of sounds. The exhale of relief and the dropping of the shoulders upon entering. The smiling faces and warm greetings from everyone, whether it is your first time here, ever, or your first time that day. Primary-red locs and honey brown twists swing over shoulders as hearty laughs clink like champagne toasts, immediately followed by cognizant apologetic whispers. The latter didn't happen before the Sign was imposed.

Jolly's experience 70 years ago is, sadly, not unlike mine. During Orientation Week 2014, white students stormed the halls of a residence building dressed like the Klu Klux Klan. There's no official record of this because the Black students who tell me they witnessed it were in first year and didn't know their rights.

A year later, using the hashtag #BlackOnCampus, our Black students brought attention to anti-Black racism on campus, such as when a Black student was solicited for marijuana (still illegal then) by strangers. In response to their truths, they were called "monkeys" and "slaves" by their colleagues on social media. Racist art depicting the students was posted on Twitter. I think of the McCarthy-esque aftermath of the protests, during which Black students on campus said they were questioned about the unrest, at random, by faculty and staff. I think of the lack of substantive change by the administration, despite its promises.

But why would the University of Guelph be any different from the rest of Canada? Contained, controlled, and surveilled, Black people only inhabit space insofar as we are allowed in this country. It's a truth that's been analyzed shrewdly by poet, writer, and theorist M. NourBeSe Philip, who hypothesizes Blackness as a phenomenon that must be contained by sanctions placed on Black movement. One need only look at her history of Caribana—once held in downtown Toronto, now relegated to Lake Shore Blvd. and surveilled by helicopters—to see how this is manifested. And it's especially true in the context of education: remember, the last segregated school in Ontario only closed in 1965, while the last in Nova Scotia closed in 1983.

Being #BlackOnCampus in Canada makes me feel straitjacketed. Our diversity is lauded only when it is convenient. Simultaneously suppressed and tokenized, you ask, who am I in the schema of my peers? Claire Huxtable? Raven Baxter? Rastus? Do I assuage their fears? Or am I a troublemaker, an agitator? What model of Blackness should I shape myself around?

As I walk in or out of the GBSA, I frequently enter into

the european forbids the african language; forbids her her spirituality; forbids her her gods; forbids her her singing and drumming; forbids her the natural impulse to cling to mother, father, child, sister and brother—forbids her family. leaves her no space. but that of the body. and the mind. which in any event they deny.

— M. NourbeSe Philip, "Black W/Holes: A History of Brief Time"

dialectic with the Sign. Sign, I am mindful of our neighbours. I shrink myself for them the second I leave the room, my papier-mâché shoulders deflating, taking in only what air they leave behind. You needn't remind me whose comfort matters more. It's as if the Sign knows that having a space to call our own lends itself to free expression, to power of sound, to making our presence known.

I'm anticipating comments that insist I am overreacting. That we must just be louder than other clubs, that the sign was added in a vacuum where anti-Blackness does not exist, and how hard is it to be courteous, anyways? But I walk past licensed pubs on campus every day. The noise emanating through their doors is significant, and has not ceased or decreased in the three years I have been here, despite close proximity to offices and lecture halls. There are no Signs asking that this happen, either.

To many folk, "keep the volume low" might seem like an innocuous request. But to those whose efforts to place-make are consistently curtailed, whose voices undergo constant erasure in the classroom, these words border on insidious. We have one room to ourselves, in a basement, several buildings away from the mainstream campus life organizations. Our voices are policed *even in this room*, disallowed to extend beyond its confines.

Keep the volume low.

It echoes the sentiments of the Canadian ministers travelling to the American South to regretfully inform Black sharecroppers that our soil cannot sustain crops or livestock, to dissuade them from immigrating here. 1908: The volume is controlled.

It echoes the era when Lake Erie was flanked by "sundown towns"—all-white cities where Black persons were forbidden from staying after sundown. 1930: The volume is controlled.

That's the same era during which 75 Klansmen burned crosses in Oakville to prevent a Black man from wedding a white woman, and were lauded for acting "quite properly" by J.B. Moat, then mayor. 1930, again: The volume is controlled.

GBSA is more than just a room. It is an opportunity to divest from the chronic inauthenticity that marks my life, and the lives of so many Black Canadian students like me. We eat our mosaic of meals together at lunch. We FaceTime relatives back home, and whether we are expats or Canada-grown, we feel guilty that we fall short of their expectations. We reminisce about coin laundry and chores under the watchful eye of our mothers, and speculate about what awaits us after convocation. We fashion space for ourselves and fulfill our ancestors' wildest dreams. Provided, of course, we keep the volume low.

12

On Fried Chicken, Disordered Eating, and Storytelling

This is a piece I wrote and delivered on June 20, 2019, at the LIGHT Stories event in Kitchener, Waterloo. This opportunity was made possible by my wonderful friend Carolina Miranda. Carolina created space for me to explain the creative process behind my writing of The Cook Not (Even) Mad, Or, Womanist Cookery: Unpacking Antiblackness In Canadian Food History. My cookbook, which was published through the Guelph Black Heritage Society and has since become my pride and joy, is available for purchase.

My name is Laila El Mugammar. I am a Sudanese Canadian woman, archives worker and amateur chef. I am here because I love fried chicken.

I am here because Rita Martin was a corporate character created in 1938 by Robin Hood Flour. A Canadian Betty Crocker, her name was chosen because it was equally pronounceable in English and French. Mary Blake. Marie Frasier. Aunt Jemima. I am here because my path has been blazed by generations of fake women. What does it mean when a man says 'real women can cook' while clutching that bottle of syrup punctuated by the smiling face of a mammy, ever ready to sate his hunger? What does it mean for me to stand here and call myself a cook? What does it mean for me to stand before you and call myself an author?

I am here because somewhere between the embarrassment of middle school graphic tees and the widened hips and parted lips of my freshman year at Cameron Heights, I declared war on my body. The physical act of taking up space made my face heat up. And so I began the arduous project of starving until it felt like I had been shovelled out. I wrapped the bitter parts of myself in the satin of my pointe shoes. I suppose it was destiny I would end up working in the archives. I logged so many hours in my teenage years curating my own body, committing every freckle and scar and stretch mark to memory. I decided which details I would omit from the exhibit of me. I scanned my meals in TIF format and catalogued the calories. I left the house wearing so much more than clothes.

I am here because somewhere between the double suite on the second floor of Lambton Hall and the publication of my cookbook at the Guelph Black Heritage Society, I signed an armistice with my body. I learned to love the expanses of soft, stretched skin, the hyperpigmentation under my arms and between my thighs, the cream-coloured stripes on my flanks. This was in part because I started my job in Archival and Special Collections at the University of Guelph, where I work with the culinary collection. We have cookbooks dating back to the sixteenth century, through slavery, confederation, the world wars, up until the present day, and my job consists of scanning and digitizing these cookbooks to meet professional librarian standards. Nothing made me appreciate the food that surrounded me more than seeing what people used to do with Jell-O! Even more nauseating than the savoury jello was the portrayals of women, Black people, and Indigenous peoples. Women were reduced to waistlines and tasked with keeping their husbands smiling and their deep freezers full. It was then that I had what my sixth-grade teacher Ms. Melissa Reist termed the "aha moment" - this history did not happen in a vacuum, and like the trickles in a champagne tower it had informed every aspect of my life as I struggled to bear weight at the bottom. This history is a laugh in the Sistine Chapel and its echoes still knock me to my knees. It raises a deafening toast to my tears and the hangover never ends. And so, almost entirely out of spite, I kicked self-hatred cold turkey. And I learned that vulnerability can be good.

I am here because food is vulnerability. We are inherently at our most vulnerable when we eat (or don't eat). We are vulnerable to poison, to disease. We are vulnerable when we cook (or don't cook). I liken cooking a meal for someone the first time as standing naked in front of them. We are vulnerable to criticism, to judgement, to sexism either way. This dichotomy that seats us between the devil and the deep blue china is a lot like other dichotomies in our lives. Clothed or unclothed, we are reprimanded and rebuked by people who are both enticed by our form and repulsed by our power. From birth, we are raised to believe that our bodies are something to be consumed. By our adolescent years we have been chewed up and spat out more times than we care to remember. By adulthood, our form committed to memory on many palettes and regurgitated to friends for a new set of judgements. Too much fat. Too spicy. The flavours too loud. Too colourful, too hot, too frigid. Too raw. Vulnerability is the word of the day, and women have been entrusted with people at their most vulnerable. In our earliest moments, eating is love, and comfort, and nourishment, and safety. Throughout our lives act of sharing a meal with someone stays incredibly intimate. Subsequently, It requires a degree of trust and it leads to a deeper recognition of need and of humanity.

I am here because food is an archive. I told you all earlier that I love fried chicken. This is true. However, as a Black woman I avoid eating fried chicken in public lest an onlooker make a minstrel out of me. I am here because slaves were allowed to keep their own chickens by law and because it was easy to fry outdoors without compromising the cooking; an asset in the oppressive heat of the American South. I am fear because of *Birth of a Nation*. I am fearless in rewriting the recipe and reimagining the history as one of resilience and glee. I am seeds of watermelon smuggled from Africa, with dreams of one day growing home. The resistance of our mothers and grandmothers is imbibed in our food.

When I first wrote my cookbook, I shivered at the thought of including fried chicken, because I knew I didn't have the fortitude to field all of its nuances. I couldn't give readers all the information. All I could do was give them a place to start. So I concerned myself instead with the kind of story I wanted to tell, because food is storytelling. I told a story I hadn't heard before. The story I told was one of sugarcane and cayenne and buttermilk baths like warm hugs. It is a story of unity forged in the crucible of three hundred and fifty degree adversity, of nourishment where there was none to be found. It is a story of making a little go a long way.

After telling that story, I made a cake imbued with the Black and Indigenous present. I made a cake that did not require an oven or a stove, but a freezer, with canned fruit and graham crackers and other pantry staples. I baked without baking, which is to say, I made do with nothing, like many who live beneath the low-income cut off do, especially up north. Cake is a celebration food, and it is hard to believe it's so inaccessible to those impacted by poverty. I made a dish that could be put outdoors in the winter and enjoyed in kind.

The last story I told was my own. This was one of peanut and lime and herring. My recipe was one of pungent smells and colourful spices. My story as a Sudanese Canadian is poutine and beavertails and Kraft Dinner as much as it is *kisra* and *molokhia* and *shai be'laban*. Assembled, these make the mosaic that is me.

For too long, we have seen food as something to simply be extracted from the land. Food is the land between your thumb and forefinger. Our history is not in our food. Our history is our food. Our food is our history. And just like history, food needs us to stay alive.

I encourage you to go forth from today, unpack the history, question the documents, and eat the food. Be skeptical. Taste the land.

13

On Cultural Renaissance

On Gaukel Street in Kitchener, Ont., perpendicular to city hall, a black bear greets pedestrians with watery and speculative eyes. *Makade Makwa.* Near her, a frog crouches, its back glimmering and pale in the sunlight. *Omakakii.* Beside him, a wolf lifts a slender snout to serenade a star-filled sky. *Maengun.* These animals are brought to life in modern, muted renderings on the painted pavement by illustrator and muralist Luke Swinson, a Kitchener resident and member of the Mississaugas of Scugog Island First Nation. His murals live on the street and on social media, where Swinson provides the Anishinaabe names for the subject of every work. An LRT ride away from the bear and her friends, fish illustrated in vibrant cyan swim freely through flora, circling a golden sun. According to Oneida artist Alanah Jewell, the mural represents "community, ceremony and belonging." In addition to being the artist behind *Morning Star Designs,* Jewell is also the

Parks and Engagement Associate for the City of Kitchener. Her goal is to connect with other Indigenous people, organizations and leaders to understand how Indigenous people would like to access park space and land. Her art can be seen reclaiming public spaces across southern Ontario.

On the other side of the continent, a similar placemaking is occurring. Black railway porters stand at the ready, waiting to service an oncoming train. They are part of a continuum of Black entrepreneurs, musicians and athletes illustrated in glorious colour, inhabiting 45 m of the side of the Dunsmuir Viaduct in East Vancouver. *Hope Through Ashes: A Requiem for Hogan's Alley*, by muralist Anthony Joseph, was born during the Vancouver Mural Festival in September. The work gives permanency to the memory of Hogan's Alley, a historically Black settlement in Strathcona that was levelled in order to make space for Vancouver's viaduct system. Joseph reclaims the viaduct and, in doing so, resurrects the Black presence where it had been so violently expunged. The master's tools contest the master's house. As of 2018, the viaducts were slated for demolition in favour of a ground-level road system, and over 12,000 residents—a quarter of whom are in social housing—are expected to inhabit the new "Hogan's Alley" that will emerge.

These are just a couple of glimpses of the blooming cultural renaissance being spearheaded by Black and Indigenous people in Canada.

Though Black people have been settled in Canada for centuries, historical accounts of Black life are largely missing from our national narrative. We inhabit the negative space of the cultural mosaic, our history slumbering in the cracked and yellowed grout between the Underground Railroad and Aubrey Drake Graham. From Hogan's Alley to Africville in Halifax, there has always been a vested effort to restrict Black placemaking in Canada. Black Canadians have always resisted this. Robyn Maynard's *Policing Black Lives* and Desmond Cole's *The Skin We're In*, which both reveal the grim realities of Black life in Canada, are national bestsellers. Black Canadian writers such as poet Dionne Brand and theorist M. NourbeSe Philip now appear on many high school and university syllabi. The movie rights to *They Said This Would Be Fun: Race, Campus Life, and Growing Up* by the young Black writer Eternity Martis were sold at auction to Boat Rocker Media. I myself was published, though I never thought it possible. I optimistically hope that going forward, credence is given to Black intellectuals and artists whose work disrupts the idea of Canada as a racism-free space.

And while government policy continues to retrench Indigenous placemaking in Canada, Indigenous writers and artists continue to prevail. The works of Tuscarora writer Alicia Elliott and Inuk writer and throat singer Tanya Tagaq were made compulsory reading during my time at the University of Guelph. The continued brilliance and resilience of Indigenous writers transcends parochial constructs of age and genre. *We Are Water Protectors* by Carole Lindstrom mobilizes kindergarten students to stand up to the "black snake" whose venom "burns the land" and makes the water unfit to drink. Katherena Vermette's graphic novel series *A Girl Called Echo* disrupts linear time and makes historical events such as the Red River Resistance accessible to youth. Volume 3 was released this year, and I eagerly await Volume 4 in the year ahead.

I am still unsure where I fit in this burgeoning cultural renaissance, but the sense of belonging I feel makes me overwhelmed with gratitude. The Canada emerging is one where I am visible. I only hope that, in 2021, this rebirth and reclamation of physical and intellectual space in the arts will flourish, and that new generations of artists continue to be inspired by the strength and resilience of our predecessors.

14

On New Orleans

The strangled cry of a Maine Coone on this Boeing 767 is my reckoning. *We live in strange times.* I think I am jet-lagged and dreaming up Biblical bellwethers when a woman sits next to me, sneezing ostentatiously. She tells me that her seatmate brought his cat in a carrier and that she is terribly, terribly allergic.

"A Carolinian, you know. An evacuator." She gesticulates and stage whispers. I feel a stir on my right. X is fidgeting.

"This is probably the first time anyone has evacuated *to* New Orleans." He adds, half asleep.

The plane departs from Hartsfield-Jackson, crowded with this quarter's climate refugees. We watch Hurricane Florence dance the Coda on the tiny televisions. The Maine Coone monologues. We eat packaged cookies and drink ginger ale. The Maine Coone monologues. *We live in strange times.* By the time we reach Louis Armstrong International, she is Ophelia in her grief. We leave the airport as the palm trees bend and sway under a green sky. Like low flying planes in New York City.

Our AirBnb host Lou is gracious and hospitable as he shows us the double-gallery house. His wife, a Haitian-initiated Voodoo priestess, decorates the walls with blessings.

"These blew off our house when Katrina hit," he explains, gesturing to the mosaic of tile that covers the coffee table. "But we Orleanians repurpose our tragedies." I tell him about the Maine Coone and the twirling storm.

He drops his voice to a whisper, as if presupposing a punitive gaze in his own home. "We thought we had it bad because Bush was president. But now. God help them."

We nod silently and he leads us to the bedroom. I trace my fingers on the water line, cresting just under my eyes. I wonder how hard I could have kicked before it swallowed me.

We drive in pursuit of crawfish. FEMA search codes emblazon building after guild, thirteen years post-disaster. Katrina crosses, as the locals call them, delineate the rescue squad, the date and time, the hazards, and the number of bodies inside. X tells me they are a badge of honour for some who survived. The GPS tells us to turn left. We can't. What our blue Ford Mustang convertible thinks is a passable street is instead an ecosystem of discarded rubber and porcelain. A canopy of overgrown weeds nestles the refuse.

We pass cemetery after cemetery. In August of 2005, the flood raised the dead. Louis Cataldie, the Emergency Medical Director for the State of Louisiana, was quoted as saying "Coffins were torn out of mausoleums like a child's blocks." Close to one thousand coffins were displaced in the storm. A two-ton concrete vault found completely submerged in a marsh contained the body of a victim of Hurricane Audrey, which struck in 1957. Skeletons were found in front yards and the city struggled to piece together the departed. I'm told that save some plaster damage from debris, the sugarcane barons were safely flanked in Saint Louis Cemetery No. 1.

We see several Creole cottages on the way to plantation country. House raising is a popular industry in the area, compounded by Katrina. The homes are elevated several stories on concrete stilts, with anxious eyes fixed on the levee.

A weathered Orleanian named Garrison meets us for po'boys. We drink in the street out of plastic cups. He tells us about the hospital that opened after the storm. He regrets to inform us it is only at thirty percent capacity.

"That's bad, because hospitals are in the business of making money," He takes a long drag of his clove cigarette and reads my face before finishing.

"At least in America, they are."

I go to recycle my plastic cup and I can't. I make a noise like the Maine Coone. We live in strange times.

I am at a bar in Vacherie, Louisiana, desperately trying to find internet and submit an assignment. Fox News, which, if you haven't had the pleasure, could also be called the Tucker Carlson Show, plays unchallenged. The host's furrowed brows pollute my line of sight as a loud headline fills the screen.

METEOROLOGIST DEBUNKS LINK BETWEEN CLIMATE CHANGE AND EXTREME WEATHER

Tucker Carlson invites a meteorologist to slander Bill Nye The Science Guy. He explains that Nye's greenhouse effect experiment designed for primary school students was "cleverly faked". The experiment features carbon dioxide entombed in a mason jar, which warms quickly when positioned under a lamp.

"He's not even a scientist. He's an engineer of some sort." The meteorologist says. I wonder if I am also a meteorologist. I laugh so hard I snort before reevaluating. I read the room. We are just outside New Orleans, the little blue pebble in the red hobnailed boot. I see knuckles whitening around Pabst Blue Ribbon. I feel myself overheating. The patrons watch the screen intently. A burly white man alerts the bartender, who nods and leans forward, hand hovering over a second PBR.

"Turn that shit off, now."

I feel like sobbing. *We live in strange times.*

fiction

15

The Body

The body was found Easter Sunday in a car on Superior Street, not on the side where Jennie Jr. lived, but on the side of the abandoned rubber factory. The car was a steel gray two-seater, and it bore the name "Ray's Reptile Emporium." When the policeman first came to her door, he asked her and Dad if they recognized the vehicle. Dad simply shrugged his shoulders, but Jennie Jr. told the policeman all about Ray's Reptile Emporium in the next town over, where you could purchase frozen baby rats for one dollar and eighty cents or a dozen quail eggs—but no quails—for five dollars plus tax from Ray. She had started to tell him about the Clown Tree Frogs and the Mexican Milk Snakes, but the policeman simply thanked her and walked away. Jennie liked Ray from Ray's Reptile Emporium because he had a ponytail and an earring and because he let her hold his ball python last summer, but she did not like the policeman because he left before she could finish talking. The body may have been Ray, or not Ray, but it was certainly a body, covered haphazardly with a bright yellow tarp. The tarp cloaked its head, which rested against the steering wheel as if asleep. She could not see a ponytail or an earring. The driver's side door was open and the leg jutted out in a way that would be painful if it were attached to a living person, and not a body. The leg was not entirely obscured by the tarp, and she could see a denim pant leg and a glossy loafer attached to the business casual body.

Police cruisers blocked Superior Street from Sebold Avenue to Twist Way. The ambulance and fire brigade came and went, and the paramedics looked at the body and shrugged before closing their big ambulance doors and driving off.

"If you're going to sit outside, you can't interfere with the policemen. They're going to set up a tape barricade - a line - that you can't cross. Don't go past that line. Do we have an agreement, Jennie Junior?"

Jennie nodded, and she and Dad shook on it. She sat on her porch while her arms got cold to watch the body. The policemen laughed with one another and avoided eye contact with her. A man whose jacket said CORONER stepped out of a Black Audi by the Sebold blockade and exchanged his warm gloves for latex gloves, which he accidentally dropped on the pavement and then slipped back on when he thought no one was looking. A man with a neck strap that said NIKON took pictures with a bulky, angular camera. The flash illuminated the street and the body in its yellow dressing. A big van that said FORENSIC IDENTIFICATION UNIT drove in front of the body and blocked it from view. The policeman arranged a line of flimsy yellow tape suspended on poles around the FORENSIC IDENTIFICATION UNIT, and Jennie deduced this was the barricade Dad told her about. She could see three sets of steel-toed feet from underneath the big white van, bathed in cyclical rounds of red and blue light. The feet danced around the body as the camera bulb flashed and the yellow tarp crumpled to the floor. Their words, on occasion, crept around the van to her. Words like "heart attack" and "dee-oh-EH" that the men stuck to the body like a "My Name Is."

When dad came to the porch to give her a blue freezie and a three-cheese Pizza Pocket, she asked him why the body was dressed in yellow. Dad explained that the body was not ready to be seen yet. He said that like Zsa Zsa Gabor - whom she had gone in costume as to the Thompson Rivers Primary School Halloween Dance - bodies needed special makeup and special clothing before they were ready to be seen by people. She imagined the body, torsoless and headless, dancing around at the Halloween Dance, smearing Ponds on its denim pants with disembodied hands, and gluing false eyelashes to its loafers to prepare for the eyes of the adoring crowds. She giggled with a mouthful of hot cheese and dough. Dad warned her to be careful so she wouldn't choke before he went back inside.

She wanted to open her blue freezie, but the smell in the air made her question it. The men said the body had been there for days and that was why it smelled like a public toilet. When she went to Grandma Jennie Sr.'s funeral, Grandma Jennie's body smelled like cleaning solution. Dad explained that the Eby Mortuary workers cleaned her body on the inside and the outside so she wouldn't make anybody sick. Grandma Jennie Sr. did not have a yellow tarp or denim pants or loafers. She wore a powder pink skirt suit and white stockings and shiny Mary Janes, with a single white dahlia in her boutonnière. Her eyebrows were thin and round like a cartoon, and her wrinkled lips looked painted on with the Russian Red lipstick she always wore before she became a body. Jennie Jr. heard Dad say that cigarettes were coffin nails, so she checked the shiny corners of Grandma Jennie's casket to see if the Palmers she loved were fastening her in. There were brass screws and squares instead of Palmers. Maybe someone had mistaken the brass for the orange butt of the Palmers, or maybe there were none because this was a *casket*, not a coffin, and caskets have different rules, or maybe there were no Palmers left in the world because Grandma Jennie smoked them all. Jennie Jr. was only seven at the funeral, and she didn't even cry when she saw her Grandma Jennie in the open casket. Dad was so proud of her; he told her so as he strapped her into the booster seat on the way home. She didn't tell him it felt like there was damp sand in her throat, or that she was angry at Grandma Jennie Sr. for smoking all the Palmers in the world. She was sad that they couldn't play another game of blackjack together, and that Grandma Jennie couldn't go with them to Mount Vernon that fall. Jennie wondered if the body in the car had ever been to Mount Vernon, but she knew better than to ask.

She heard one of the men retch from behind the van. Jennie Junior wondered if she should tell the CORONER to go to the Eby Mortuary so they could make the body smell nice and so no one else would get sick, but he was behind the yellow tape. Dad and Jennie Jr. had an agreement that she could watch everything unfold as long as she didn't interfere, and in their previous discussions, he told her giving advice was interfering.

When the street lights finally turned on, she realized the feet had stopped dancing. They had moved to the side as she saw a big, heavy shadow move from the Ray's Reptile Emporium car into the van. She noticed the way the black lines in the broken road carved into the old asphalt, like veins under the feet. Many people thought this was tar, but Jennie Jr. knew that it was a high-performance polymer-asphalt blend, designed to preserve what was left by sealing the cracks. She wanted to tell the policemen and the body to be mindful of the bumpy road with the polymer-asphalt mix, but they had already moved the body into the van. She heard two big slams, and the van drove away, but not before the driver hollered "AND CALL THE DAMN TOW TRUCK!" at the policemen. Jennie flinched and shook her head at what she and dad called a "poor word choice."

Even though the body was gone, the car that said "Ray's Reptile Emporium" was still there. The driver's side door was wide open, and without the body obstructing the view, she could see a rosary on the dashboard. The beads looked wooden, big, and heavy. There was a light brown stain on the driver's seat and a newspaper on the vestibule. Aside from that, the car was much emptier than her and Dad's: her booster seat took up a lot of space.

Dad opened the screen door and beckoned for her to come in.

"It's bedtime, Jennie Junior. Say goodbye to the body."

Jennie shook her head. "The body's gone. The tow truck still has to get here and take away Ray's car."

"The tow truck won't be here for a while," Dad responded patiently. "You have to brush your teeth and go to bed."

Jennie shrugged her shoulders and went inside.

Works Cited

"Oh, How She Did Suffer": On Displacement and Contestation in the American West
For Dr. Christine Bold, ENGL*4420 01 Women's Writings F20, 30 November 2020

"Aristotle's Rhetoric." *Stanford Encyclopedia of Philosophy*, Edited by Edward N. Zalta, Centre for the Study of Language and Information, 2010.

Cesaire, Aime. *Discourse On Colonialism*. Aakar Books, 2018.

Kleist, Jacquelynn. "Sarah Winnemucca's 'Life Among the Piutes: Their Wrongs and Claims' as Captivity Narrative." *CEA Critic,* vol. 75, no. 2, 2013, pp. 79–92.

Lamont, Victoria. "Introduction." *Westerns: A Women's History.* University of Nebraska Press, 2016.

Lape, Noreen Groover. "'I Would Rather Be with My People, but Not to Live with Them as They Live': Cultural Liminality and Double Consciousness in Sarah Winnemucca Hopkins's 'Life among the Piutes: Their Wrongs and Claims.'" *American Indian Quarterly*, vol. 22, no. 3, 1998, pp. 259–279.

O'Brien, Colleen. "'"All the Land Had Changed": Territorial Expansion and the Native American Past in Pauline Hopkins's Winona." *Studies in American Fiction*, vol. 41 no. 1, 2014, p. 27-48

Patterson, Martha H. "'Kin' o' Rough Jestice Fer a Parson': Pauline Hopkins's Winona and the Politics of Reconstructing History." *African American Review*, vol. 32, no. 3, 1998, pp. 445–460. JSTOR,

On Queer Stigma And Shame in *Fight Club*
For Dr. Jade Ferguson, ENGL*2120 Critical Practices, 07 December 2018

Altman, Lawrence K. "New Homosexual Disorder Worries Health Officials ." *The New York Times*, 11 May 1982, p. 01.

Giroux, Henry A. "Breaking into the Movies: Public Pedagogy and the Politics of Film." *Policy Futures in Education*, vol. 9, no. 6, 2011, pp. 686–695.

Halberstam, Judith. *The Queer Art of Failure*. Duke University Press, 2011.

"Where Youse Belong:" On Placemaking in Black Diasporic and Indigenous Writing
For Dr. Paul Barrett, ENGL*3870 Literary and Cultural Studies, 2 December 2019

Abrams, M. H. A Glossary of Literary Terms. 7th ed., Heinle & Heinle, 1999.

Antwi, Phanuel. "Rough Play: Reading Black Masculinity in Austin Clarke's "Sometimes, a

Motherless Child" and Dionne Brand's What We All Long For" (Critical Essay)." Studies in Canadian Literature, vol. 34, no. 2, 2009, pp. 194–222.

Archibald, Linda, et al. "Documentation of Traditional Inuit Practices Related to Pregnancy and Childbirth." Journal SOGC, vol. 18, no. 5, May 1996, pp. 423–433.

Philip, M. NourbeSe. "Black W/Holes: A History of Brief Time." Transition, no. 124, 2017, pp. 118–136.

On "Brokeback Mountain"
For Dr. Christine Bold, ENGL*4420 Women's Writings, 23 October 2020

Limerick, Patricia Nelson. "Introduction: Closing The Frontier and Opening Western History." *The Legacy of Conquest: The Unbroken Past of the American West.* Norton, 1987.

Needham, Gary. "Queering The Western." *Brokeback Mountain.* Edinburgh University Press, 2010.

Halberstam, Jack. "Animating Failure." *The Queer Art of Failure,* Duke University Press, 2011

On Contact Zones, Safe Houses, and the Ahmed Mohamed Clock Incident
For Dr. Eid Mohamed, HIST2160 9/11 In Historical Perspective, 05 April 2021

Alsultany, Evelyn. "Arabs and Muslims in the Media after 9/11: Representational Strategies for a 'Postrace' Era." *American quarterly* 65, no. 1 (2013): 161–169.

"Fellow Muslim Student Defends 'Clock Kid's' Former High School." CBS Dallas / Fort Worth, December 1, 2015.

Nazia Kazi. "Ahmed Mohamed and the Imperial Necessity of Islamophilia." Islamophobia Studies Journal 3, no. 1 (2015): 115-26.

Pratt, Mary Louise. "Arts of the Contact Zone." *Profession,* 1991, 33-40.

Said, Edward W. *Orientalism* 1st ed. New York: Pantheon Books, 1978.

Smith, Kyle. "How Ahmed's Clock Became a False, Convenient Tale of Racism." New York Post. New York Post, September 21, 2015.

Taranto, James. "Stand With Ahmed: But Against The Islamophobia Mythmakers." The Wall Street Journal. Dow Jones & Company, September 18, 2015.

On Tampons, the Archive, and *Nervous Conditions*
For Dr. Julie Cairnie, ENGL*3960, Literature in History, 25 February 2019

Burton, Antoinette M. "Archive Fever, Archive Stories." *Archive Stories: Facts, Fictions, and the Writing of History,* Duke University Press, 2005, pp. 1–24.

Dangarembga, Tsitsi. *Nervous Conditions.* Ayebia Clarke, 2004.

Foucault, Michel. "Introduction." *The Archaeology of Knowledge and the Discourse on Language,* Pantheon Books, 1972, pp. 3–17.

On New Orleans
Creative Nonfiction for Dr. Martha Nandorfy, ENGL*2130 Literature and Social Change, 21 November 2018

Koppel, Lily. "Coffins and Buried Remains Set Adrift by Hurricanes Create a Grisly Puzzle." Archives: The New York Times, The New York Times, 25 Oct. 2005.

Ross, Janell. "The Art - and Controversy - of Hurricane Katrina 'X-Codes'." The Washington Post, WP Company, 29 Aug. 2015.

Acknowledgments

Thanks to Lawrence Hill for your help in navigating the publication process, and to Dionne Brand, Jade Ferguson, Julie Cairnie, Daniel O'Quinn, Mark Fortier, Christine Bold, Martha Nandorfy, and countless others for teaching me how to write mindfully. To Devon Spier for opening the door to professional writing for me.

To my wonderful friends. To my family. To every professor who has ever given me an extension on an assignment. To the good folks at McLaughlin Library. To Andrew. To everyone I've forgotten to name. To Kaitlyn Mullin who took the beautiful photo of me on the back cover of the print edition. All gratitude. So much gratitude.

Laila El Mugammar is a Sudanese-Canadian journalist and BA Honours English alumna of the University of Guelph. Her first publication "Keep The Volume Low: Being Black on Campus in Canada" was published on Chatelaine.com in May of 2020. She has since published more articles mapping Canada's historical and modern relationship with Blackness in Chatelaine, Maclean's, insideWaterloo and The Ontarion. She is also the author of *The Cook Not (Even) Mad; Or, Womanist Cookery: Unpacking AntiBlackness in Canadian Food History*, a fundraising cookbook published by the Guelph Black Heritage Society. She is a passionate supporter of libraries and archives, an ALA Spectrum Scholar, and is pursuing a Master of Library and Information Science.

© Photograph by Kaitlyn Mullin of Captured by Kait Photography.

www.ingramcontent.com/pod-product-compliance
Lightning Source LLC
Chambersburg PA
CBHW070937080526
44589CB00013B/1541